TRAVEL
DEVOTIONS

refreshing your soul with lessons from traveling

by Laura Vae Gatz

ISBN: 978-0-9831664-3-6

1. Religion - Devotional

Editors: Robert & Laura DeLanoy
Cover Design & Photographs, Interior Photographs
and Layout: Laura Vae Gatz

http://lauragatz.com
facebook.com/LauraVaeGatz

CONTENTS

For my Mother who has, in her way,
been helping me remember all kinds
of travel stories and other memories.
I love and treasure you!

AIRPLANE PERSPECTIVE

Praise the Lord from the earth, you great sea creatures
and all ocean depths, lightning and hail,
snow and clouds, stormy winds that do his bidding,
you mountains and all hills, fruit trees and all cedars,
wild animals and all cattle,
small creatures and flying birds.

PSALM 148:7-10

I've always loved sitting by the window on a plane, looking out and observing the land passing by. It's so interesting to be high up in the air with a vastly different perspective than the one I normally have each day. I am fascinated by how the land's features change as the plane flies across the country. Desert erosion patterns that look like plumes of feathers replace endless irrigated fields with their round circle patterns. Flying over the Rocky Mountains is especially exciting when the sky is clear and I can easily see mountain peaks and valleys covered in snow. The deep shades of aqua warm my soul when landing in the Caribbean. When I visited Ireland several years ago, the impossibly green fields were incredibly lush and inviting, just as I had always imagined them. Looking at this endless variety of nature reminds me of God's majesty and unmatched creativity.

This time spent flying through the air at high speeds is the perfect opportunity to reflect on God's glory. Make sure you reserve yourself a window seat! Psalm 19:1 reads, "The heavens declare the glory of God; the skies proclaim the work of his hands." God created the heavens and the earth to declare the majesty and splendor of its Creator. Being isolated on a plane with the perfect distant perspective of creation, encourages me to focus on His attributes – how intensely creative, incomprehensible, and superlative God is.

Flying through and around clouds captivates me. It speaks to my inner child who imagined zooming next to fluffy cumulous clouds like Superman, or sitting on a cloud like an angel. When the airplane climbs above the clouds on an overcast day, there is often a heaviness that lifts from my soul as we

reach that altitude where it breaks through the clouds into the sun, with the clouds now below in an endless sea of radiant white.

The next time you are on a plane and are able to look out the window to enjoy God's varied and beautiful creation, spend some time thanking Him for His spectacular and beautiful creation. Thank Him for specific things that speak to your soul; the beauty of a sunrise, the wonder of a rainbow after a storm, the stark beauty of the desert and its varied succulents, or the fragile, satin-soft petals of a spring flower.

Dear Lord, Thank You for the majesty of Your creation. I love how creative and varied it is. Each day I notice something new. Thank You for surrounding me with signs of Your presence and with beauty that reflects Your attributes. Awaken my soul to a continual awareness of Your presence through Your creation. Amen.

STRANGLER FIG

*He is like a tree planted by water, that sends out its roots
by the stream, and does not fear when heat comes,
for its leaves remain green, and is not anxious
in the year of drought, for it does not cease to bear fruit.*

JEREMIAH 17:8

When I was planning my trip to Cambodia, one of the fascinating features of the land I wanted to see were the tall trees which had roots that grew on, in, through, and around whatever got in their paths. These crazy roots would engulf buildings, and take over like squadrons of enormous boa constrictors lying on top of and hanging off of everything in sight. There are two types of trees responsible for this, the strangler fig and the silk-cotton tree.

Wandering around the ancient temples, I can almost feel the trees watching me. They almost feel alive. They are simply beautiful, tall and stately, with roots that look like lava cascading over a wall. One tree I pass looks as if it is just out for a stroll along the top of a wall. Another tree appears to pose half-way across an arch. It feels as if these trees might move around if everyone left, just like children think their toys do when left in a room alone. Other trees look like they got hungry and started chowing down on the local architecture. And others decided they wanted to BE part of the architecture, their roots appearing to hold these ancient structures together. These trees have taken over, and appear to be in charge. Their roots have infiltrated every nook and cranny of these buildings. I even saw stairs that were covered with roots; the roots followed the contours of the stairs like surface veins, changing direction ninety degrees with each step. These trees left me slack-jawed, and in awe. When I think of the temples of Beng Malea or Ta Prohm, what left its imprint in my mind were the trees.

When we become followers of the Christ, He starts to leave His imprint on us. The more we grow in faith, the more of His characteristics we start to take on. As we let God into each area of our lives, He weaves His presence into the fibers of our being. Ultimately, I hope that one day when people interact with me, what they'll really see is Christ. Although I'll be present, the most indelible memory they'll take away will be that of Christ in me. It can take a lifetime to develop the trust and faith we require to be so fully attuned to God; as God increases, I decrease (meaning that as God's influence increases in me, my will and desires take a back seat to His).

I've met people who radiate their faith. I can feel it as soon as I approach them. They almost seem to glow, or ooze God's love and grace. They often leave me with the feeling, "I want what they have!" As I spend quiet time alone with God, telling Him all that is on my heart, interceding for friends and family, asking for forgiveness for a multitude of sins, and asking for the help my heart needs that day, I frequently feel the roots of God starting to weave their way throughout my life. I feel propped up by the strength of God's love wrapping itself around the parts of me that feel like falling apart.

Dear Lord, Thank You for the fascinating trees You created. Thank You for allowing me to see You more clearly through Your beautiful creation. As I seek You each day, please continue to grow in me, suffusing me with Your characteristics. Help me to feel Your presence, and allow me to glow with Your love, grace, peace and strength. Amen.

Rough Seas

Jesus was sleeping at the back of the boat with his head
on a cushion. The disciples woke him up, shouting,
"Teacher, don't you care that we're going to drown?"
When Jesus woke up, he rebuked the wind and said
to the waves, "Silence! Be still!" Suddenly the wind stopped,
and there was a great calm. Then he asked them,
"Why are you afraid? Do you still have no faith?"

Mark 4: 38-40 NLT

Yesterday I embarked on a three-week journey on the National Geographic Explorer, a motor vessel, which will be in the Arctic Circle during most of that time. As we sailed out of the safe, quiet harbor of Longyearbyen in Svalbard, Norway, we started to encounter some rolling seas; nothing extreme, but certainly not the steady solidness of land or the gentle rocking of the protected harbor. At first, I was excited. I love to be on ships and to feel the movement of the water beneath my feet. But pretty soon I wasn't feeling well. Not one prone to experience seasickness often, I must have left both my motion sickness prevention wristbands and my seasickness pills at home. I discovered this last night as I was starting to experience the first signs of seasickness (the queasy stomach and strange feeling of being incredibly hot). As I was looking for these two things (the pills and the wristbands) I started to panic a little bit, and I thought, "Oh, no! Did I leave those at home? Why would I do that?"

For anyone who has experienced seasickness, you know the awful feeling in the pit of your stomach, literally, when you realize you're getting sick. You start to wonder how long its going to last. Is it going to get worse? Will you throw up? Will you feel like this the rest of the trip? Your mind starts to race and, on top of not feeling well physically, you start to not feel well mentally. All you want is a way out. You want it to stop.

This experience brought to mind the Bible story of the apostles encountering the storm while in their fishing boat. Similar thoughts of anxiety must have gone through their minds. How bad is this storm going to get? How long is it going to last? Will we make it through this? Their minds raced, and all they wanted was a way out. They wanted it to stop!

Life is often like this. We're sailing along and things are good when all of a sudden we hit a snag, a bump, or a big rogue wave and we panic. "Oh, no!" we think, "What will happen now?" It is at this moment that we should focus our eyes on Jesus. Just as fixing your eyes on the horizon calms the internal storms of seasickness, focusing our minds and hearts on Jesus, calms our daily storms in life.

When I couldn't find anything in my luggage that would help my queasy stomach, I had to look elsewhere. I had to rely on someone else to help me. I remembered at our orientation meeting, the onboard doctor said that there were seasickness pills at the reception desk. (That's a sign of an adventurous trip!) I ran to get a packet, took one of the pills, and lay down to relax. Within ten minutes I was starting to feel better.

When we remember to turn to the Lord during the storms in our lives, whether those storms are large or small, we will feel His Peace, the peace that passes all understanding. The 23rd Psalm says "The Lord is my shepherd, I shall not want. He makes me lie down in green pastures. He leads me beside still waters; He restores my soul…Yea, though I walk through the valley of the shadow of death, I will fear no evil, for Thou art with me, Thy rod and Thy staff they comfort me."

God is there in our storms of life to comfort us, to renew us, to give us rest, and to keep us from all evil.

> Dear Lord, Thank You for the storms in my life that make me turn to You, my one and only true Comforter and Rescuer. Thank You for Your constant love, peace, and grace that help me through rough times, and which draw me close to You, reminding me that You are my Comforter, the Restorer of my soul and the Giver of rest and peace. Amen.

Be Light

In the same way, let your light shine before others,
so that they may see your good works and give glory
to your Father who is in heaven.

MATTHEW 5:16

When I'm traveling it is easy for me to be focused only on my goal of getting to my destination, while neglecting everything else. I focus inwardly; making sure I get to the airport on time, that I make it through security correctly and quickly, not leaving anything behind. I select a seat in the boarding area that isn't too close to anyone having a loud mobile phone conversation. I watch the time and take a trip to the bathroom a few minutes before boarding. Then I get in line as soon as my group is called and make sure I find overhead bin space for my suitcase close to my seat. I sit down in my aisle seat and try to make sure no one bashes into me with his or her luggage or purse. I'm focused solely on myself. Occasionally my conscience pricks me, and I gain awareness of my selfishness and self-centeredness, and realize the matters I'm consumed with are the things of this world. I need to concentrate on the things that last eternally – like showing love and kindness, being generous with my time, and investing my resources in sharing the Gospel with others.

God calls us to be light to others and to let His light shine through us. I'm certainly not letting my light shine when I don't interact with others. My light is dim or non-existent when I'm only focusing on myself. When I've been traveling a long time, or when I'm tired or don't feel well, it may be ok to turn inward and focus on myself, but more often, I need to turn my focus outward and let God's love-light shine through me to others. Admittedly, this is not always easy for me as an introvert. It is in these circumstances I become aware that God may have opportunities for me to shine His love on others. When I slow down, I start to see possible opportunities to make a difference, even if it is a small difference. We never know how a smile or a nice gesture, such as opening the door for someone, can impact someone's day.

Often, when I'm waiting somewhere by myself, I will ask the person next to me a question which engages them in conversation. It's fun to find out information about strangers. People are interesting. As part of the natural flow of conversation sometimes I am able to share a story from my life about how I saw God work in or through me.

Be open to the opportunities God places in your path. Ask God to show you when and how to interact with strangers. He will supply you with the words to use. Prayerfully consider where God would have you invest your time and resources to make an impact for His Kingdom.

Dear Lord, Too often I find I am only thinking of myself. Help me focus outwardly, with the mission to help others, and to shine Your light through my actions and speech. Please nudge me into awareness of the opportunities you would have me pursue to further the mission of Your Kingdom. Amen.

ENNUI

These all died in faith, not having received the things promised,
but having seen them and greeted them from afar, and having
acknowledged that they were strangers and exiles on the earth.
For people who speak thus make it clear that they are seeking
a homeland. If they had been thinking of that land
from which they had gone out, they would have had
opportunity to return. But as it is, they desire a better country,
that is, a heavenly one. Therefore God is not ashamed
to be called their God, for he has prepared for them a city.

HEBREWS 11:13-16 ESV

Traveling is work. And the older I get, the more work it seems to be. I think I've become soft over the years because there are more things about home that I miss when I'm traveling; things that make me yearn for it when I'm not there. While in Mexico I really miss my soft and comfortable mattress. When making food from an RV, I miss all the counter space and special kitchen utensils I most often take for granted. When traveling for work, I miss having my favorite foods in the pantry, especially after a week of eating in restaurants. Often I just miss the comfort of being surrounded by a place I know intimately; a place that I've made my own. Travel makes me miss my home.

Sometimes homesickness sneaks up on me, and I must sit silently and think through what is bothering me before I can pinpoint that my feelings are those of homesickness. In the middle of a delightful and refreshing trip, this yearning starts to grow; I long for something else. At first, it feels confusing. Why am I not happy? Why do I feel sadness in my heart? I'm on a fabulous trip and enjoying new sights and cultural experiences; how could I be discontent? And then it hits me that I miss my home: my family, my friends, and my familiar surroundings.

I also feel this longing when I am at home. It is still a longing for home, but for a different home. Before I realize the source of the longing, I try to fill it up with things from this world: food, movies, entertainment, busyness. But those things all fail to satisfy truly. When I start looking for something to fill the hole in my heart, that longing that nothing in this world can fill, I need to realize that the hunger I am experiencing is my longing to be home, with God. This world is not my home; I am just here for a short while. Heaven is my home, and as a believer in Jesus Christ, I am programmed with a longing to be with Him all the time.

When you are traveling and experience ennui for home, use it for its unique perspective of all the blessings you have in your daily life, and to remind you that this world is not your home. Cultivate that longing for Heaven by spending more time in God's Word, and time in quietness with Him. There is nothing quite like being away from home to enable you to see and feel what it is that you love there.

Dear Lord, Thank You that this earth is not my home and that I get to be with You for eternity. When the longing comes and I try to fill my life with the things of this world, help me to see that what I am actually longing for is You; time with You, Your Word, and Your guidance and love. Amen.

In-Between

*We can rejoice, too, when we run into problems and trials,
for we know that they help us develop endurance.
And endurance develops strength of character,
and character strengthens our confident hope of salvation.*

ROMANS 5:3-4 NLTse

When I'm at the airport half way to my destination, I often feel like a person without a country, especially when my next flight has been canceled and I am stuck mid-route. I'm not surrounded by the comforts of my home, and I haven't yet experienced the excitement of reaching my planned destination. I'm tired, hungry, and yearn to be either back home or at the end of my journey. I'm in the land in-between, and that is a frustrating place to be stuck, whether it is due to disrupted travel plans or due to other disruptions in life: when we've been let go from a job and we're looking for work, as we wait for a diagnosis for a loved one's illness, or that lengthy period in the middle of a divorce. No matter the trial, the land in-between is where we do not want to be, a place between departure and destination, and is often a place of fertile soil where God grows us.

When I am in the land in-between, it feels like I'm on a desert island with no way off. I'm stuck. It's as if I'm driving down a road and I'm half way across a drawbridge. While in the middle of it, the drawbridges on both sides go up, trapping me. Because I'm not surrounded by the comforts of home I can't rely on them, they're not available. I also can't depend on the distractions of my destination because I'm not there either. My lack of options forces my attention to God. I can't improve things on my own. I must admit I cannot function alone. I must draw near to God and whisper in His ear that I am insufficient for this task. I can't do it on my own; I need Him. This is sweet music to God's heart. He yearns for us to need Him. He longs for us to get to the end of ourselves so that we reach out to Him.

The Israelites could relate to this time of waiting. They spent forty years in the desert, their land in-between. I doubt when they left Egypt they thought an entire generation would pass away before they arrived in the Promised Land. God had a purpose for them in the wilderness. He needed time to grow them into believers who trusted in Him, changing them from the idol worshipers they'd become during generations in Egypt. They needed time to learn to trust Him through the many ways God showed His faithfulness by providing for their needs in the desert.

While waiting in the wilderness, things got a little boring and they started to take for granted having their needs met. They ate manna for breakfast, lunch, and dinner, over and over. Although they weren't hungry, they were sick of manna and whining about it as it says in Numbers 11:4-6. They needed to learn how to be content, and to ask God to give them peace and patience.

To be content where you are, say, "For now, this is where I am and what I am doing." This is it for NOW. It won't last forever. God has a purpose for me in this trial. Be thankful in the midst of a time of waiting. When I am discouraged and not enjoying the place in which I am waiting, I thank God for this challenge and pray that He would use it to bring me closer to Him and to enable me to open my heart to Him, to recognize and accept that I can't do it without Him.

> *Dear Lord, I am so often overwhelmed by my circumstances and need Your help. Thank You for being my constant companion, always there to assist. Open my heart to confide in You, to admit to myself and to You that I can't do it on my own. Grow my trust in You to bring me through my current trial and to learn the lesson you have for me in it. "I can't Lord; You can!" Amen.*

HANOI ROAD

I have set the Lord always before me;
because He is at my right hand, I shall not be shaken.

PSALM 16:8

Before I took my first trip to Vietnam, a friend of mine who had been there gave me some sage advice, which I didn't fully comprehend until after I'd arrived. My friend told me that to cross the street there, you had to look at the traffic coming and then step out into it, walking at a steady pace. I thought that was a little odd. Crossing a street wouldn't be a challenge.

When I arrived in Hanoi, and headed out for my first excursion, I quickly came across a very busy one-way road. Buses, motorcycles, mopeds and rickshaws were all hurtling down the street, with no lanes apparent. There were no stoplights or crosswalks, just an endless stream of chaotic traffic. At intersections, the traffic just merged from all four directions, like a tangle of opposing armies, except they didn't run into each other. Somehow each lane made progress. I laughed at the impossibility of crossing a road like that! And then I remembered my friend's advice to look at the traffic, keep your eye on it, and step off the curb, keeping the same steady pace. Don't increase or decrease your speed. I took a big breath, said a quick prayer for safety, waited for a few busses to pass, and then I stepped off the curb into the chaos.

I looked motorists in the eye as I walked perpendicular to them, willing them to see me, willing them to make course corrections so we wouldn't collide. I kept my pace steady even though I wanted to run. The road seemed very broad, and I felt like I'd never get to the other side. I knew the safest way through this maze of danger was to stay steady, and not to rush through.

Just as there was no safe way to rush across that road, there is no way to rush through an ordeal full of mental or emotional distress. The length and breadth are determined by God and by His Will, but if we keep our eyes on Him, He will walk through it with us and will protect us along the way.

God promises in Romans 8:28 for those who love Him, that He will use every circumstance, every challenge, every rough spot and every valley, to benefit us. What we need to do is to keep our eyes fixed firmly on Him, inviting Him into each moment of our day, focusing on Him and not on our problem. By walking steadily with Him, He will see that we make it safely through.

Dear Lord, So often I feel as if my life is like crossing that road in Vietnam; trouble just keeps coming, and everything feels scary and dangerous. During those times, please help me to keep my eyes fixed on You. Instill in my heart the knowledge and trust that You are with me every step of the way and that You are using each challenge to benefit me. Amen.

Hard Bed

*Not that I am speaking of being in need, for I have learned
in whatever situation I am to be content. I know
how to be brought low, and I know how to abound.
In any and every circumstance, I have learned the secret
of facing plenty and hunger, abundance and need. I can do
all things through him who strengthens me.*

PHILIPPIANS 4:11-13

It is nighttime, and although I should be sleeping, I am not. I am awake, ruminating about the unusually hard surface that is my bed tonight. How can people sleep on a mattress this hard? I feel like I'm sleeping on concrete. In fact, I am – the foundation for this futon-like mattress is a solid concrete platform about thirty-six inches high. For some reason, many places I stay throughout Europe have hard beds, and it drives me crazy. Not being able to sleep, especially after a long day of travel, makes me grumpy and petulant. Lying here irritated, I realize that I'm not helping my situation. My irritation will never make this bed softer. And while I'm lying awake, using my time to worry about the details of my trip isn't going to solve anything either, it's simply going to drain me of energy, of which I already feel depleted.

It dawns on me that I've been running in high gear for weeks, too busy to slow down and spend time with God. These hours awake in the middle of the night are a perfect opportunity, possibly even orchestrated by God, to put me in a position where my best option is to talk with Him.

My perspective starts to swing around from irritation to gratefulness. Although I'm still tired and weary, I open my heart to God and start telling Him about what I'm concerned and worried about. I can choose to waste this time tossing and turning, worrying and wishing I were asleep, or I can talk to my Creator and Father and unload my cares and worries. 1 Peter 5:7 says "Cast all your cares on Him for He cares for you." This invitation is always open, and God is always waiting for us to take the time to speak with him. Even though He already knows what is on our heart and mind, He desires for us to show our trust in Him by confiding in Him.

Once I've told God everything that is weighing my heart down and making it sad, anxious, or fearful, I praise Him for who He is: for His constancy, love, peace, and grace. I thank Him for sending Jesus to die for my sins so that I am transformed into a forgiven sinner, which makes it possible for me to talk directly to Him. I thank Him for specific blessings in my life, and even the challenges, which never fail to bring me to my knees seeking Him and His refreshing peace. And lastly, I examine my heart for what troubles it and ask God specifically to cure what ails it. Very often I pray for peace, freedom from fear and anxiety, and that I would be able to extend His grace to others. When I've finished, I find I am content to lay awake and be in His presence. I don't feel the hard bed anymore. God has superseded my circumstances.

Dear Lord, Please help me to more fully comprehend that You want me to cast all my cares and worries on You. I know You don't want to see me stressed out; that You're waiting by my side to carry my load. Help me to be content through any circumstances, to not let troubles weigh me down. Refresh me and strengthen me according to Your Will. Amen.

PRAY BOLDLY

So I say to you, ask, and it will be given to you; seek,
and you will find; knock, and it will be opened to you.
For everyone who asks receives, and he who seeks finds,
and to him who knocks it will be opened.

LUKE 11:9-10 NKJV

I don't know about you, but I like to get the same entrée at restaurants I visit frequently. When I go to church I try to sit in approximately the same spot I usually sit in; it's comfortable. When I take a vacation, it's effortless to return to a place I've been before and loved, the same city, hotel, restaurants. We are typically creatures of habit, and we like the familiar and comfortable; somewhere we are at ease. When I spent a semester in Germany during college, a lot of my free weekends I traveled to and stayed at the International Youth Hotel in Salzburg, Austria. I liked it there, felt comfortable, liked the city, and the food was fantastic and inexpensive. I got to know many of the staff. It became my home away from home. Years later when I traveled with my sister, we mostly went on Windjammer sailboat cruises again and again because we enjoyed them and knew what to expect. The older I get, the more I like to be comfortable, travel to a place already familiar, and the less I like to be adventurous and try new things. I don't like to trust that something new will be good, or even better than what I already know.

We tell ourselves that sticking with the familiar is shrewd. We tell ourselves it is the safe option. And maybe as we age it's not altogether a bad idea to travel to familiar places, but in our lives, we need to pursue the dreams God calls us to. We're reluctant to want more, worried it won't be as good, it will be hard, or we are afraid it will be a miserable failure.

We are often content with what we have. Is seems good, and it is comfortable. We don't want to be open to more because it is scary. Being content with what we have is good unless God is calling us to more or something different. Our contentedness can leave us with a smaller, less brilliant, version of a bigger, more vivid life that God wants to give us.

God has a plan for our lives, to give us more than we ever could imagine, however, to realize (live) that life, we have to be open to the opportunity, trust Him, and step out in faith.

The Bible is filled with people who God called to take on larger roles than they'd ever dreamed, or even wanted, but they each had a significant impact for God's Kingdom. Moses faced Pharaoh and lead the Israelites out of Egypt. Nehemiah, Artaxerxes' cupbearer, was called to rebuild Jerusalem's wall after it had been abandoned for years. Jonah was called by God as a missionary to save Nineveh; a task he didn't want. The Ninevites were idol worshipers and had been a threat to Israel for a long time. He knew God's plan was to be merciful and he didn't think they deserved it.

For me, stepping out in faith has taken many forms. I've stepped out in faith to write devotional books. I very strongly feel God's leading to write and to share the gospel with people I may never have a chance to meet in person, through my writing – writing that God guides. I also felt God's guiding to do some public speaking. Whenever an opportunity presented itself, I accepted even though I was scared, apprehensive, and secretly doubtful how I could positively impact anyone through my meager speaking skills. However, I also knew that if that was where God wanted me, He would enable His words through me to reach His intended targets. He also does this when I talk to strangers in the airport and during my travels.

Dear Lord, Inspire me to pray boldly to know Your Will. Help me to pray with my heart, not just my mind. And when I can't summon the words, I'll pray with tears and groans trusting the Holy Spirit to intercede on my behalf. Thank You for the amazing gift of Your Holy Spirit to help us out when we can't put our agony into words. Help me to be open to Your guiding hand. Amen.

GREED

A greedy man stirs up strife, but the one who
trusts in the Lord will be enriched.

PROVERBS 28:25

When I was sixteen, I was part of a Rotary Exchange program. I spent three weeks in Germany with a family, and at the end of that time, their fifteen-year-old son came back to America with me to spend three weeks with my family. One night we were having dinner together on their back porch, surrounded by a beautiful garden with a koi pond to one side. The mother brought out a huge bowl of fragrant smelling meat and sauce. It looked like beef stroganoff. As the guest, she encouraged me to take food first, and I dug into that bowl, carefully trying to make sure I got a lot of meat. I was hungry and was being greedy. When we started eating, I popped a piece of meat in my mouth eager to taste it, and as soon as I bit into it, I realized my error.

This meat was not beef, but liver. I hate liver! My mind started racing as I tried to maintain a somewhat calm appearance until I decided what to do. As a guest, spitting out the food would have been rude. Not eating it would also be just as rude. I was either going to eat the liver or fess up and admit that I just don't like liver. I looked at my plate in dismay. There was no way I was going to be able to eat all that liver. Why had I been so greedy? I might have been able to eat a few pieces by employing a children's age-old secret of combining an icky food with something tasty and swallowing it quickly. But there was no way I was going to be able to choke down all that liver on my plate.

I was very embarrassed but decided the only way out was to admit I'd taken so much because it looked so good, and explain how much I dislike liver. What a humbling experience. Now as an adult, it can still be tempting to be greedy sometimes, perhaps taking too much at the church potluck because that one dish looks and smells so good. Rarely does that ever turn out well. Taking a little is usually the right course of action. Why do I get greedy?

There are two main reasons: I'm only thinking of myself, and I think, "If I don't get it now, there won't be any left later."

I think our society encourages this line of thinking. Advertising touts looking out for number one, getting while the getting's good, and self-reliance. Jesus's philosophy ran counter to culture. His message was and is to love each other, which translates into thinking of others first. That is where God calls our hearts to be. He also wants us to trust Him for provision. We don't need to be so concerned about providing for ourselves because He will provide what we need, and even more so if we're focused on serving and loving others above ourselves. Our preacher put it this way the other week: if we're grasping all we can get with both hands, we don't have a hand free to receive gifts from God. We need to hold less tightly to what we think we need and open our hands and hearts to receive what God desires to give us, which is always better than what we could imagine for ourselves.

Dear Lord, When I'm being greedy, prick my conscious to be aware of it, and give me a yearning to change. Please work in my heart to refocus my energies on putting others first. Help me to love others, placing their needs above my own, and trusting You to take care of my needs. Amen.

INCONSISTENCY

The counsel of the Lord stands forever,
the plans of his heart to all generations.

PSALM 33:11

've just gotten through the security gauntlet at the airport, again. Oh, how I miss the days when going through security wasn't much more than a second thought. Those days seem so far gone. I'm reminded of them when I watch old movies where friends meet each other at the end of the jet bridge as one of them exits a plane that has just flown in from somewhere far away.

These days it seems the rules for what you can and cannot carry through security change constantly. Sometimes even if the rules haven't changed, I find the security folks somewhat inconsistent regarding what is allowed in my carry-on luggage. I used to travel with a miniature screwdriver set containing interchangeable tips. The screwdriver was only a few inches long, and I flew with it for years. One day as I went through security they pulled my bag for closer inspection and removed this screwdriver set. They said I could keep the screwdriver itself, but they confiscated the tips, which were each less than an inch long. Other times I've forgotten to take scissors or a pocket knife out of a backpack I use when I'm not flying, and upon arriving at my destination, I discover the contraband still inside, undiscovered by security. Inconsistency must be part of what makes us all human. We simply can't count on anyone reacting the same way every single time in any circumstance. It can make life a little confusing. But God is consistent. He never changes, and that is so comforting.

The Bible is full of passages that proclaim our God's consistency, His unfailing love, and His unchanging nature. Psalms 136:1 (NIV) declares God's unfailing love, "Praise the Lord. He is good. His love never fails." Hebrews 13:8 (ESV) says "Jesus Christ is the same yesterday today and forever." James 1:17 (NLT) says "Whatever is good and perfect is a gift coming down to us from God our Father, who created all the lights in the heavens. He never changes or casts a shifting shadow." And Psalms 102:

25-27 reminds us that God created a world that changes but He remains the same, "Of old you laid the foundation of the earth, and the heavens are the work of your hands. They will perish, but you will remain; they will all wear out like a garment. You will change them like a robe, and they will pass away, but you are the same, and your years have no end."

Everything in my world seems to change constantly. The apps on my iPhone change their features, function, and icons frequently. Operating systems change, resulting in new features to learn. The weather changes, sometimes several times in one day. As soon as I find a pair of shoes I like, the manufacturer changes the style. At work, my boss changes, my responsibilities change, and processes change. As we age, our bodies and minds change too. It has been said that the only constant is change. But not where God is concerned. God is the only constant.

In a world where we can hardly count on anything staying the same, what great assurance it is to know that God is the Rock we can rely on to never change. His rules don't change. The degree to which He loves us never wanes or changes. In Malachi 3:6 God says, "I the Lord do not change..." From this we can understand that each of His attributes are eternal, unchanging. God is a perfect example of unwavering dependability. God will love us, guide us, and hold our hand throughout our entire lives if we will let Him.

Dear Lord, In this world of unending change, it fills my soul with peace that You are unchanging. That throughout the ages, even though rivers change their course and mountain ranges come and go, You never change. You loved me yesterday, love me today, and will love me forever. Thank You for being the one constant in my life, and help me to comprehend just a fraction of what that means. Amen.

TRUST

Listen! The LORD's arm is not too weak to save you,
nor is his ear too deaf to hear you call.

NUMBERS 11:23 NLT

Toward the end of the safari portion of my stay in Africa, I had one last safari camp to visit. During this last trip, I would cross the border at a river, from Botswana to Zambia. It included transportation by Jeep, plane, boat, microbus and walking. Every other trip involved only flying from camp to camp, taking off and landing at the small grass or dirt runways at each camp. This last trip felt like a bit of a mystery to me. I did not understand how it was all going to happen. I had arranged my safari through a company whose specialty is organizing safari trips for tourists, and they had made all the transportation arrangements. All I had to do was show up at the lodge's airstrip on time. Although I did not understand all the details of how I was going to get from one lodge to the next, I trusted God to keep me safe and make it happen. I had spent much time praying for this day, and finally put it all into God's hands, knowing I had no control over the outcome. Looking back over the duration of my trip, I could see how God had kept me safe throughout. I spent my day in calm anticipation, waiting to see how the day would turn out.

I did know what the first few steps of my transportation entailed: flying from the lodge to the town of Kasane, and then waiting at the airport for a gentleman to call my name. He would then drive me, in his Jeep, to the border. I waited a long time. Finally, someone called my name. That man drove me to the border between Botswana and Zambia. Trucks lined the road leading to the border for several miles. I asked my driver why they were all there. He said that the Zambezi River was at flood stage, which drastically slows down the one-truck ferry that takes the trucks across the river. Some of these trucks had been waiting weeks to get across the river.

I showed my passport to the customs agent in a small white trailer, had my passport stamped, and then boarded a small row boat with a motor, pointed out by my driver. When I asked what happened on the other side, he only said, "Someone will be there to take you to where you are staying tonight." So I trusted my driver's directions and the company that set this up, and got into the small boat with the stranger at the tiller, and we slowly crossed the very full, swiftly flowing Zambezi. There was a gentleman in a microbus who was there to pick me up. About 20 minutes later we were driving down the dirt road where my last safari lodge was located. I'd made it safely.

When you're traveling and face unknown factors or situations that could potentially put you in harm's way, turn your circumstances and the outcome over to your Savior. Trust Him to guide your steps, keep you safe, and to open your eyes to opportunities to shine His light into the lives of all you meet along the way. The path may not be the one you'd planned to travel, but God's way is always better than any path we could plan for ourselves.

Dear Lord, Thank You for the opportunity to have adventures while traveling. When dangers appear to loom on the horizon, help me to trust You to see me safely through. Use these difficult situations to draw me closer to You, develop my confidence in You, and enable me to draw on Your strength, patience, and grace. Amen.

Airport Woes

Whoever exalts himself will be humbled,
and whoever humbles himself will be exalted.
Matthew 23:12 ESV

The airplane boarding area is very loud this morning because there is a large group of teenage girls sitting together, around forty of them. Two security guards walk by me as they comment, "Boy, that is going to be one loud flight to Denver!" I respond back with, "Yeah, I'm glad I'm not on it!" I think to myself how loud and boisterous they are. After a week of cleaning out and packing up my parents' Arizona home, I'm just too tired to deal with that much external energy and noise.

About twenty minutes later as I'm standing in the boarding line, I hear a gate agent announce over the intercom, "Will Laura Gatz (and he really mispronounces my last name) please come to gate six for immediate boarding?" I'm thinking, "I'm already here!" So I ask the gate agent next to him, "Why did that fellow just page me? I AM here." He says he doesn't think he paged me and asks if I have a boarding pass and then just tells me to get back in line. Moments later I hear them page me again. I wave my arms in the air to the same guy that told me to line up, and he says, "Your gate is over there! They're waiting for you." So I run over to the next gate, which has no line and only the gate agent standing at the door. He says he is glad I made it, and that it is a full flight. Unbelievable! I can't believe I was standing in the wrong boarding line. That's a first.

I give my boarding pass to the gate agent and start walking down the jet bridge. About twenty feet down the jet bridge, I've caught up to the end of the line of folks waiting to board the aircraft. I look behind me and there is no one. I'm the very last person to board the plane. That rarely happens - only when I'm running late from a delayed flight or short connection.

"God - You always take care of me, even when I'm being dense, prideful, or stupid," I whisper to God mentally. God is always faithful to provide.

He watches over me no matter what. Whether I'm puffed up with pride or feeling like a loser, He directs my steps.

Upon boarding, I find a seat and a spot for my luggage, all in the 5th row. Divine intervention! My layover in Denver is about a half an hour, just long enough to make my next connection, if we are on time, if the gate is close, and if I'm not in the back of the plane.

The woman seated next to me is headed to San Francisco and we started talking about where we are from and the challenges of life. An idea formed in my mind to give her one of each of my devotional books, which I did. I think she was touched and said a few times how "It was good timing." I'll never know how those devotions may have spoken to her, but I'm so glad that I listened to that still small voice that urged me to gift her with the books.

And guess who is on this plane? All those teenagers! And they weren't loud or annoying at all.

Dear Lord, You always watch over me no matter how blind, dense, or arrogant I am. You turn every day events into opportunities to advance Your Kingdom, if I'm paying attention. Help me to see and act on the opportunities You lay before me. Use me to bless others I meet as I travel, and in my day-to-day life. Amen.

le Tre Sorelle

Come to me, all you who are weary and burdened,
and I will give you rest. Take my yoke upon you
and learn from me, for I am gentle and humble in heart,
and you will find rest for your souls.

MATTHEW 11:28-29 NIV

At mid-day, after roaming the stair-stepped streets of Positano, Italy, we are ready for a respite from the crowds. Our feet are tired and our throats parched by the warm summer Mediterranean air. Close to the water we spy a restaurant with plentiful outdoor seating, conducive to people watching while resting in the shade; le tre Sorelle.

This lovely restaurant was originally opened in 1953 when Positano was still a small village of farmers and fishermen, and tourists were just starting to discover this little gem of a town. Sisters Giovannia, Adeline and Nannina opened this restaurant, using a wood oven to bake their homemade bread. It is still family-owned today. This location adjacent to the beach, gives us ample time to observe passers-by, watch the street artists painting the famous coastline, and enjoy a cappuccino and chocolate profiteroles.

I find that the time I spend in a place while relaxing, is the time I most fondly remember, and yet I so often find it difficult to slow down. I think we've been trained by society, advertising and TV to stay in continuous motion. I can remember more clearly the times I've stopped in a park to sit on a bench and observe the landscaping, flowers and visitors. The day my husband and I visited Ravello and the gardens there, what I remember most fondly is the hour or so we stopped to rest on benches that were shaded by flowering vines and overlooked the coastline. We had a snack, rehydrated, and talked about our day as we watched visitors stroll by.

This practice of rest is one of the things God seeks for us. God wants us to rest from work. "Six days do your work, but on the seventh day do not work, so that your ox and your donkey may rest, and so that the slave born in your household and the foreigner living among you may be refreshed." (Exodus

23:12, NIV) God wants to give us the gift of stillness. "Be still before the LORD and wait patiently for him …" (Psalm 37:7, NIV) He desires us to rest from busyness and have time to recharge. "Then, because so many people were coming and going that they did not even have a chance to eat, he said to them, "Come with me by yourselves to a quiet place and get some rest." (Mark 6:31, NIV)

When I travel, I've observed that my fondest memories are those from times of rest. This affects how I build my itinerary. I build in downtime. I might schedule one or two destinations or goals for the day, but then let providence guide the rest of the day. In my experience, what good is travel if you don't have time to explore the side-roads and enjoy cafes you encounter?

My downtime during travel also gives me opportunity to pray, thanking God for the day and the fascinating place I find myself in. I have time to experience His goodness by drinking in the creativity of His creation, demonstrated in the beauty of nature: the rocks, fields, streams, trees, animals and flowers.

> *Dear Lord, I thank You for Your desire of rest for me. I appreciate the rest I receive when slowing down during travels. Thank You for enriching that time for me, and for deepening my memories so that I crave rest. Encourage my heart to seek You during times of rest, and open my eyes to the beauty of Your creation and how it declares Your glory. Amen.*

VALLEYS

*Even though I walk through the valley of the shadow
of death, I will fear no evil, for you are with me;
your rod and your staff, they comfort me.*

PSALM 23:4

Today we visited the church in Rennebu, Norway, just up the road from our Bed & Breakfast, the Meslo Herberge. The Austrians who had spent the night there too had started walking there before we were ready to leave. They took what is known as the Pilgrim's road up on the side of the hill. From there is a good view of the valley, and they could see the church while they were still a long way off. Norway seems to have a strong culture of pilgrimage, where people walk from Oslo to the church in Trondheim. This pilgrimage is similar to the pilgrimages people do in other parts of the world, to Israel or along the Appian Way. The Austrians said, as they arrived, that the way they walked was a good way to walk because it helped them keep their mind on the goal of their walk, getting to the church, and thinking on God.

This makes me think of life. Sometimes when we are in the middle of the valley we can't see God. Sometimes, in order to get a little perspective, we need to be walking along the side of the hills on either side of the valley. From this vantage point we can see how God is with us in the valleys of life. And from their perspective, along most of their walk, they could see the little Lutheran church in Rennebu, down the valley a ways; the steeple sticking up like a guiding beacon or a lighthouse. That's the way life is if you're paying attention. When you're not in the middle of the valley it can be easier to see that God is already there in the valley waiting to walk alongside you when you arrive there. Isn't it always easier to see what's really going on when you have some distance from a situation? After repeated experiences looking back to see how God always walked with you in the middle of each valley, you know that He's there even when you can't see or feel Him.

The 23rd Psalm reminds me "Though I walk through the valley of the shadow of death, I will fear no evil, for thou art with me, thy rod and they staff they comfort me."

Father in Heaven, Thank You for giving me perspective on my life. Thank You for so clearly being with me during my darkest times. Help me to keep Your constancy in my heart when I'm back in the middle of the valley. Even when I can't feel You, instill Your peace in my heart, calm my fears, and help me to cling to You always. Amen.

GREEN PASTURES

*The Lord is my shepherd; I shall not want. He makes me
lie down in green pastures. He leads me beside still waters.
He restores my soul.*

PSALM 23: 1-3A

I had a window seat on the plane the first time I flew into Ireland. As our plane descended into Shannon, I looked out the window and saw a beautiful patchwork quilt of bright green fields divided by rock walls. I had imagined Ireland would look like this, and seeing my hopes fulfilled was thrilling. When traveling to a new place I never quite know if my expectations will be met, if the picture in my mind will match reality, or if Hollywood and my imagination only fabricated that image. These green fields were everything I'd imagined, and the sight of them soothed my soul and gave me joy.

When I read the 23rd Psalm, particularly the line where God "makes me lie down in green pastures," it is those green fields of Ireland I picture. Sometimes dotted with sheep, those pastures invite peace and restoration into my soul. There's just something about a sea of green spreading out before me, with gently rolling hills in the background and waist-high rock walls built from the rocks farmers have found in these fields throughout the centuries, that say peace to me.

In much the same way, spending time by a stream in Colorado is soothing to me. Listening to the sound of water rushing over rocks, small waterfalls forming as water cascades over large boulders, takes my mind off whatever is troubling in my life. One of my favorite places that stands out, a place where I can just be in the moment, is a place called Wild Basin trailhead by Ouzel Falls, between Lyons and Estes Park on Route 7. Being surrounded by nature and the fresh damp smell of a thick layer of pine needles on the forest floor all works to remind me of the goodness of God, His infinite creativity, and how He craves to care for me and refresh me, body, soul and mind.

God is our great shepherd, seeking to keep us safe, guide, protect and restore us. As you travel, find time with your Savior. Spend quiet time with Him in nature. Search for places that rejuvenate you, where you can glory in His creation. Use this time away from home, often our only time without those extra "household" responsibilities, to allow God to refresh you.

> *Dear Lord, Thank You for Your marvelous creation. You are such a blessing to me; having You as my loving and guiding shepherd. Help me make a point, as I travel, to seek out beautiful places where I can spend quiet time with You and seek Your restorative hand. Amen.*

LATE

Not everyone who calls out to me, 'Lord! Lord!' will enter the Kingdom of Heaven. Only those who actually do the will of my Father in heaven will enter.

MATTHEW 7:21 NLT

I heard a woman in the airport security line, just ahead of me, frantically talking with the TSA agent. She was arguing with him that she should be allowed to go through the special, shorter TSA line (which we were in) even though her boarding pass was not stamped with the words "TSA pre-check." She had counted on being able to go through the short line and had arrived at the airport too close to takeoff time. Now she did not have time to wait in the regular, longer security line. The TSA officer calmly explained her options, but the woman just kept repeating, "I don't have time, I will miss my plane," as if that could change the facts or the rules. She wanted the rules to change because she had not planned appropriately. She wanted to shift the responsibility from herself to someone else.

I had just experienced a similar issue with my boarding pass. Catching her before she left the line I explained how I had taken care of the same problem, hoping it might allow her to catch her plane. But when I explained what to do, she only said, "I don't have time, I will miss my flight," and walked off. The little voice in my head silently commented, "You don't have time not to." Fixing the problem would take much less time than waiting in the extremely long security line. But I was unable to help her.

I think many of us walk through life in the same mindset as the frustrated woman. I often find myself wanting others to make an exception to the rules for me, believing that I am an exception to the rule; that somehow I am special. And I am special, to Jesus. But although He thoroughly loves me and prays for me, he cannot make an exception to the rules, especially when it comes to where I will spend eternity. He will only save me if I believe He is God and came to earth as Jesus to die on a cross as a substitutionary sacrifice to save me from my sins. If I don't believe that, and have not accepted Him as my Lord and Savior, He cannot save me from eternity in Hell, and I will not be with Him in Heaven after I die.

Sometimes I imagine a long line in the afterlife just as we arrive, kind of like the security line at the airport. Those of us who think we are going to Heaven get in the shorter line. But for many, when they get to the credential-checkers at the front who will look to see if they have been stamped with the seal of Christ, they will be found without the required seal. All of those who don't have it will have to get in the long line to Hell. I can just imagine some of the arguments of those who are turned away. "But I always went to church!" Or, "I was a good person." Jesus says in the Bible that He will say, "I never knew you," Matthew 7:23. A few verses earlier, in Matthew 7:21, it reads, "Not everyone who calls out to me, 'Lord! Lord! Will enter the Kingdom of Heaven, only those who actually do the will of my Father in heaven will enter."

Eternity is a long time, something unfathomable to my mind. Although it seems far away and unreal, deciding where I will spend eternity is the most important decision I can make in this life. I've entrusted my life to Jesus Christ. Read John 3:16 (NLTse) and decide if it applies to you, "For this is how God loved the world: He gave his one and only Son, so that everyone who believes in him will not perish but have eternal life." Examine your heart and make sure you have not only mentally accepted Christ as your Savior, but accepted Him into your heart as well. When you love someone, you want to follow their lead, their will.

Dear Lord, It is so hard to realize that whether I believe in You and what Jesus came to do here on earth, affects where I'll be forever. Sometimes it just doesn't seem real. Keep my eyes and heart focused on You, give me the desire to seek Your Will and do it, and show me opportunities to share this Good News with strangers and friends. Amen.

REFRESHED

The heavens declare the glory of God;
the skies proclaim the work of his hands.

PSALM 19:1 NIV

Leonardo da Vinci said, "An average human looks without seeing, listens without hearing, touches without feeling, eats without tasting, moves without physical awareness, inhales without awareness of odor or fragrance, and talks without thinking." Our Heavenly Father desires so much more for us. He desires that we enjoy His creation, experience joy and peace from it, and glorify Him through it.

When I have been feeling disconnected and dull, I often look for rejuvenation – a reawakening. Sometimes I find it in sitting still in the sun as I soak up the warmth and feel peace spread throughout my body. Or I find life and renewal in seeing the beautiful aqua of the Caribbean waters up close, in a broken China plate piece tumbled by the water, or in colorfully patterned fish found while snorkeling. We all go to the beach to search for something: inspiration, a breath of life, some change, interesting rocks or shells on the shore. Fishermen are looking for fish. Folks with metal detectors are looking for a bit of forgotten treasure. Surfers are looking for that perfect wave. We are all looking for a spark of life.

As I get older, I find it harder to see something as if I'm seeing it for the first time, with awe and wonder as if through a child's eyes. I miss being able to experience such amazement so effortlessly. But if we open our minds and our hearts to the possibility and seek amazement, we will be able to experience it more often. I've seen such profound beauty in a milkweed seed floating through the air, how it looks like it is lit internally. I'm completely captivated by the moment and experience. My mind follows the floating seed as it follows the wind, rising, falling, and twirling until it drifts out of sight. Then I come back to myself and realize I was lost in the moment and mesmerized by God's amazing creation. I have paused to soak in the stunning beauty of a flower, spellbound by the intricate and delicate design of its petals. Again, I'm fully in the moment, experiencing a moment alone with God through His creativity. I remember standing on our back deck at sunset, entranced by a vibrant color in the sky that infuses me with wonder, confused as to why I've never noticed its beauty before. These brief experiences are gifts to us from our divine Creator, moments of refreshment. I experience them more often when I've been spending consistent daily alone time with Him, pouring out my heart, my inadequacy to cope, and my great need for His support, love, peace, perseverance, and joy.

God desires to rejuvenate us in our life now and in our life to come in heaven, where everything will be new each day. Our Heavenly Father created everything to reflect His glory and to teach us who God is. Job 12:7-9 ESV says, "But ask the beasts, and they will teach you; the birds of the heavens, and they will tell you; or the bushes of the earth, and they will teach you; and the fish of the sea will declare to you. Who among all these does not know that the hand of the Lord has done this?"

Seek to experience God in His creation fully. Take time to go for a walk, sit in a park, literally smell the roses, lie on a blanket and stare at the sky or the stars, and be fully present in the moment. Find your way of receiving God's creation as a gift.

Dear Lord, Thank You for Your spectacular creation, and for the ways in which it can speak to me. Open my heart and slow my pace to receive Your blessings and refreshment through the creation I interact with, and work within me to be fully present in the moment. Amen.

SOLO

*Then Peter called to him, "Lord, if it's really you, tell me
to come to you, walking on the water." "Yes, come," Jesus said.
So Peter went over the side of the boat and walked on the water
toward Jesus. But when he saw the strong wind and the waves,
he was terrified and began to sink. "Save me, Lord!" he shouted.
Jesus immediately reached out and grabbed him. "You have
so little faith," Jesus said. "Why did you doubt me?"*

MATTHEW 14:28-31 NLT

I'm in the midst of my first trip to Asia. I've visited Vietnam and Cambodia
and am at Siem Reap International Airport, awaiting my next flight, to
Taiwan. The day started out great. My ride showed up on time – the
same tuk-tuk and driver I've been riding around with all week. So it was
a pleasant drive, sitting in the open-air carriage with my luggage snuggly
beneath my legs. We even saw two large sleeping pigs tied upside-down on
the back of a motorbike on their way to market. My driver said that the pigs
are given alcohol before the ride so that they don't mind the ride so much.
I've never seen anything like it!

I'm so early that the ticket counters aren't even open yet. So I sit outside
and buy a cold young coconut with a straw and have a drink, along with an
almond croissant. Yum! Fresh, warm, and flaky. Things are looking good.

But my day and confidence start to deteriorate when I try to check in at
the airline counter. They don't have my ticket. I made all my reservations
through one airline, but on this leg, I'm flying one of their partner airlines.
They say they see my ticket but can't check me in until they can talk with
the airline that booked it with them, and that counter doesn't open for
another hour, fairly close to when my flight departs. It's going to be pretty
tight timing if I'm going to make my flight. My calm has melted away, and
now I'm just beside myself with worry. What if they can't fix the problem in
time? How could this have happened? How are they going to fix it?

I hate feeling powerless over this situation, and it sounds like there's nothing I could have done to prevent it. But I don't give up easily. I figure out how to use my mobile phone to call the airline that made my airline reservations to see what they can do for me while I wait. The more I try to work the problem, the more frantic I get. I call home and cry to Mom. I ask her to pray that it all works out. Then there's more waiting. My mind is racing and my heart is beating fast.

Why did I think I could make this trip all by myself? It had been going so well! When traveling alone, the only person you have to rely on is yourself. You have to do everything yourself, including hauling your luggage into the tiny bathroom stall when using the facilities! God, help! I need help. I can't figure this out on my own.

It is only when I realize I can't do it on my own, and I ask for His help, that God rescues me. If I don't ask for help, he won't answer my unspoken need. He wants me to realize my need for Him and blesses me when I admit I can't do it alone. When I am small, God is large. When I am empty, God fills me up. When I cry out, God comes in.

God uses tough times like these to bless me, but I have to be open to the blessing by inviting Him into my mess and admitting that I need help. Being afraid opens up space inside of myself, for Him. God wants me to rely on Him. He wants me to ask boldly, in His Name (consistent with His Will, His Word, and His character) for what I need. And to ask with the right motives – to advance His Kingdom.

Dear Lord, Thank You for blessing me with the ability and means to travel. Thank You for being right beside me all the way, waiting until I realize my need for You, so that I ask for Your help when things start to go badly. Thank You for filling me up when I am empty, for rescuing me and keeping me safe through all circumstances. Remind me to rely on and trust in You, always. Amen.

OVERPACKING

*Their destiny is destruction, their god
is their stomach, and their glory is in their shame.
Their mind is set on earthly things.*

We all have a tendency to pack too much. When I think I've packed lightly, and have returned from my trip, inevitably there are clothes I didn't wear and items I didn't use. I've always told myself that's ok because I'm packing for "what if." What if it is colder or warmer than the weather forecast? What if I get allergies and need medication? What if I need an Ace bandage because I twist my ankle? I am a master "what if" packer. I try to anticipate any eventuality and bring items that will meet that need, especially if my trip is taking me to remote areas. Of course, this leads to too much luggage and bulkier, heavier bags.

I've had a dream, however remote, of someday hiking the Appalachian Trail. Because I like to read and research other peoples' experiences, I've read many books written by those who have hiked it. One common hiker experience is packing items that aren't necessary. One of the first few overnight stops serves as an "unloading station" where hikers reevaluate their needs. When you're carrying everything you need to exist, on your back, the definitions of "need" and "want" quickly change. That big book of nature poetry is quickly tossed on the "not required" pile. The saw for cutting firewood, the umbrella, and the camp chair all become extraneous items. Cheryl Strayed, who hiked the Pacific Crest Trail started out with a huge backpack, which affectionately became known as Monster, weighing in at 53 lbs. Once she'd whittled it down to only necessary items, it weighed 35 lbs, still pretty significant, but much more manageable.

In life, we all tend to pack too much stuff for "what if." We try to guarantee preparedness for whatever comes our way, ensuring that as much as possible we are self-reliant. Even young girls are taught to be ready for anything; the Girl Scout motto is "Be Prepared." We surround ourselves with things and services meant to stave off disaster: AAA for a flat tire, home insurance for fire or tornado damage, car insurance in case we get in an accident, escape ladders for second-story windows in case a fire blocks our exit, candles or generators in case the power goes out. In and of themselves, those services or things are not bad, but when we come to rely on them wholeheartedly instead of leaning into and relying on God first, those things can become gods.

Sometimes the first glimpse we get of what it truly means to trust God is when all the things we've come to depend on have been stripped bare: our house is wiped out by a tornado, the biopsy comes back malignant, our spouse dies unexpectedly, we lose our job. Whatever it is that destroys our sense of self-reliance and causes us to lose all hope, is often the same thing that causes us to call out to God in desperation knowing that our earthly assurances have failed us. Once God has gotten our attention and shown us His love by getting us through the storm, we need to start reaching out to Him in all areas of our lives, not just when things have gotten terrible. Self-reliance is a myth we sell ourselves.

Edward Mote says it best in his hymn, "My Hope is Built on Nothing Less," which refers to the parable of the wise and the foolish builders. The chorus goes, "On Christ, the solid Rock, I stand; All other ground is sinking sand." These words enforce that only in Christ are we safe and secure. In the second verse he says, "In every high and stormy gale, My anchor holds within the veil." My anchor during storms is Christ, and He is holding me within the veil – referring to the Holy of Holies, the most sacred of places, and eternal life with Him. And the third verse, "When every earthly prop gives way, He then is all my Hope and Stay." The definition of a prop is an object placed beneath or against a structure to keep it from falling or shaking; a support. When our earthly props, the things we surround ourselves with thinking they'll allow us to be self-sufficient, fail, it is then that He is all my hope and support. Stay refers to the rope that supports the mast. God is our support always, and especially when everything else fails.

Dear Lord, Please forgive me for relying on earthly props which eventually fail. Thank You for always supporting me, for keeping me safe with You for eternity, and for being my Solid Rock, always. Remind me to lean on You during every trial and storm in my life, and to lean on You first, not just when I have nothing left to lean on. Amen.

IRRITATIONS

*For those who live according to the flesh set their minds on
the things of the flesh, but those who live according to the Spirit
set their minds on the things of the Spirit.*

ROMANS 8:5

When I travel, especially on an airplane, I find myself getting irritated at people for not being as aware as I think they should be. For example, the person who grabs the back of my seat to steady themselves as they get up, often pulling my hair, or the person who reclines in front of someone with really long legs who doesn't quite fit in the seat. Or the person who walks down the aisle, bumping everyone sitting on the aisle with his/her large shoulder bag. It is easy to get aggravated with others, and stay focused on how inconsiderate I think they are, instead of turning the spotlight on myself. I need to change my perspective and stay focused on my actions, ensuring that I do not inconvenience someone else. When I focus on others' actions, I tend to behave like the folks who are irritating me. When I focus on my own actions I act more like the Christ.

How can I help others when I am traveling? Can I lift a bag up to put it in the overhead compartment for someone else? Can I help a tired mother by distracting a fussy child? Can I help direct a traveler who seems lost or out of sorts? Maybe it's as simple as complimenting the server at the coffee shop or the cleaning crew in the bathrooms for the great job they do. Whatever actions I choose to take, I should be aware that those encounters are chances to shine God's light to others.

One trick that has helped me in so many circumstances throughout my life is to always assume positive intent. That means that when interacting with others I believe the best of them instead of the worst. Instead of thinking they ran their bag into me on purpose, I choose to trust that they were concentrating on more important matters. Instead of thinking they meant to be rude, I pray for them in case they're going through a trial or having a rough day. This practice works at home too. When my son is grumpy, instead of taking it as a personal offense, wondering what his problem is now, I go to him lovingly and give him a hug. It takes conscious effort, especially on difficult days, but if I can help to create a family that always assumes positive intent, it makes a huge difference in everyone's life.

Pray for God to extend his peace, love, and patience to you and to all you do and encounter throughout your day. Ask for Him to open your eyes to opportunities to shine His light in others' lives by giving them the benefit of the doubt and assisting where possible.

Dear Heavenly Father, This can be a challenging and difficult world to live in. Please help me to change my thoughts about others by being more positive. Help me to be compassionate, to look for opportunities to assist others, and to accept irritations with the help of Your grace. Amen.

PORTHOLE

For I know the plans I have for you, declares the Lord,
plans for welfare and not for evil, to give you a future and a hope.
JEREMIAH 29:11

'm on a ship headed for the Antarctic. We are sailing across the Drake Passage later today; a section of water south of South America notorious for its severe and unpredictable weather and large swells. I am a little apprehensive about the crossing. This is the first leg of a two-month sabbatical, and I'm wondering what I've done. I'm feeling nervous and out of my element.

After breakfast this morning I came back to the cabin, opened my laptop and played Twila Paris's song, "God is in Control." I just love that song. It has such powerful lyrics. Whenever I am experiencing anxiety or confusion I like to play this song in private, and just belt out the words, singing along.

So this morning, while alone in my cabin, I've got the speakers up as loud as they'll go and I'm singing the lyrics at the top of my lungs. To paraphrase the artist's lyrics, "Don't fear now, have faith and resolve, keep on with your mission, don't give into sentiment, grasp what you've hidden in your heart, one thing will always remain true, it keeps the universe cohesive. The Lord is in command; we trust that He won't ever desert his offspring. God is in control, we elect to recall this and not be traumatized. God remains beside us. He is in charge."

It is so assuring to sing these words. God IS in control. I believe this. It is reassuring though to sing it over and over. It grounds me. No matter what is happening in my life, I know that God IS in control. One of the verses says, "He has never let you down, why start to worry now?" And that is so true. I think we forget how faithful God is. He has never let me down, why would I worry now? Sometimes I am so ashamed that my faith seems so small, and then I get back into the Word and spend time with the Lord, and I start to see so clearly how God is beside me all the way every day. God IS in control!

When I'm feeling God's control, it makes me feel like a small child in the backseat of our family car. I know that Mom and Dad are in control, taking care of me, and making sure I stay safe. If I fall asleep before we reach home, they'll gather me up in their arms and carry me inside to my bed and tuck me in safe and sound. And as their child, I completely trust them, which is why I can fall asleep before we reach home. There is no doubt in my mind that they'll be there for me. Why is it as adults we so often logically believe this but when difficulties arise we want to take back that control from God and not rest in His loving arms? I'm going to strive to be more like a little child letting the Lord wrap his arms around me and tuck me into bed safe and sound.

When you feel anxious or out of control, visualize God wrapping His arms around you like a parent does with a child, and soak in all that comfort and love.

Dear Lord, Thank You for loving me so thoroughly and comprehensively, for being my Father in heaven, for always wanting the best for me. Help me to surrender to You, seek Your guidance and support, devote time each day talking with You and spend quiet time in Your presence. When I feel unsure or afraid, help me to feel Your loving arms wrapped tightly around me. Amen.

Too Hot

*For in six days the Lord made heaven
and earth, but on the seventh day
he stopped working and was refreshed.*

Exodus 31:17b NLTse

I'm on a hike with my family in Utah in the summer, and it is blazing hot. The route I'm walking is down low in a wash, where water runs when it rains. Today the wash is bone dry. On a sunny day, the washes are hotter than the higher ground because breezes don't reach down into the crevasse, and because the heat from the walls reflects back into the wash, making the air hotter. I don't feel like walking any farther, I can't bear another step; I just can't do it mentally or physically. I feel like this hike is going to go on forever. I'm done!

I sit down under a slight overhang in the shade, to wait for my hiking companions to return. Once I've stopped moving, I become aware of what surrounds me: the slight breeze, the heat, and the deep blue sky. In the silence, I can sense God. I take off my hiking boots to empty out the sand and pebbles which have accumulated, take off my socks to let them dry out and then put them back on.

I'm attempting to recover my attitude. The high today is supposed to be 103°F. It's 11:42 AM and the temperature is close to that already, but there is no way to know for sure because there is no mobile coverage out here southeast of Kanab, in the southwest part of Utah. It feels hot enough to fry an egg on the sand, but I don't have one of those either. I look out to the sun-bleached wash beyond the shade of my overhang, and I think of the Israelites out in the desert for 40 years. I'll bet it was hot. They didn't have any air conditioning!

Currently, I'm irritated because the RV we are renting now has a problem with its generator, which means no air conditioning while we are camping. There have been many other issues with this camper; all relatively minor, but cumulatively they mean the camper is not being well maintained. I had not minded all the little things, but this generator issue has pushed my attitude over the edge.

Aren't we often like those RV owners though? We let small issues build up for a long time, and we don't do regular maintenance on our faith or relationship with God until something major happens. We don't pray daily or spend time with God, as we would with a close friend, until we hit the rocks and feel like it's just not possible to keep going and we don't have anywhere else to turn.

Sitting here in the heat, I can identify with the Israelites in the desert. They were most likely hot and weary, discouraged by not being settled, worn out, and probably somewhat worried. Personally, when I'm hot I am easily irritated, and I'll bet they were too. They wanted to be refreshed: a cold drink of river water, a meal that wasn't made of manna, some time alone from the enormous crowd.

God always provides. If I let Him, God will be a cool drink of water for me and will give me the ability to keep going. I just have to tell Him how I feel, then admit that I am not capable and that I can only do it through His strength. I just whisper "Lord Jesus," when I can't go on anymore. The Holy Spirit will intercede on my behalf if I don't have the words. If I do have the words, I tell God how I'm feeling, and what I need. I admit I'm not able to do it on my own, and I ask for help. God doesn't care if our words are well thought out, He just wants us to be totally honest and to admit we can't do it without Him.

Dear Lord, Some days are just so hard, and I feel like I can't go on. Help me to stop worrying and talk to You throughout my days. Open my heart to share with You how I feel. Encourage me to admit that I can't do it alone and to ask for Your assistance. I ask that You would enable me to give up worry and fear and to always look to You to provide peace and love through all of life's circumstances. Amen.

CROSSROADS

Stand at the crossroads and look;
ask for the ancient paths,
ask where the good way is, and walk in it,
and you will find rest for your souls.

JEREMIAH 6:16 NIV

've driven in several foreign countries. From driving on the left side of the road to figuring out what all the different traffic signs mean, I've enjoyed the challenge and experience. I love how narrow the roads are in Scotland and Ireland, and that there is no room to swerve for a pothole. And there aren't many because the climate is more temperate than northern Michigan; much less freezing and thawing. I thoroughly enjoy the narrow twisty roads with a rock wall on one side, and who-knows-what bearing down on you from the other direction.

When I'm out in the countryside, driving along enjoying the view, I love it when I come to a crossroad, fork in the road, or a T-intersection, where there are multiple signs indicating how far it is to towns in each direction. If no one is behind me, I like to pause to read each sign and imagine what I might find at those locations. What mystery might each town hold: a quaint café for a cup of tea, or a beautiful ocean-side park with an unusual path? Maybe I'd discover an old family pub with great atmosphere and a smoky peat fire to keep the occupants warm. Which way should I go? What am I in search of? Do I have an itinerary to follow or am I just out wandering for the day?

I know the signs are directional and placed there to help people find their way, but I think they're also picturesque, and I like to take pictures of them. They remind me that I'm in an area where I don't know my way around; somewhere foreign. The names of these towns are not familiar to me. I wouldn't know what to expect if I went there.

God calls us to stand at the crossroads and seek guidance. These crossroads are places and times in our lives where we have to make decisions; the proverbial fork in the road, a T-intersection with a selection of options from which to choose.

God would have us choose the way of godliness and righteousness. What options would honor Him? We should choose carefully. Pray about it. Read the Word and meditate on it. Seek God's counsel and ask for His wisdom. Choose what will further His Kingdom and His work here on earth. Ask everything in the name of Jesus, and in His Will and His timing.

> *Dear Lord, My life is filled with crossroads. Help me to select the correct option each time, the one that will glorify You, and further Your work here on earth. Help me to think about eternal consequences and not just immediate gratification. Remind me that my actions while I'm alive affect my eternal life forever. Amen.*

PRIDE

When pride comes, then comes disgrace,
but with the humble is wisdom.

PROVERBS 11:2

I've been in Arizona for almost a week and am flying home tomorrow on Southwest. Because of Southwest's open seating policy (seats are not assigned), I need to check in for my flight 24 hours before departure time if I am to get a decent spot in line and avoid boarding in the last group. Southwest assigns me a boarding group and position in line once I check in. The earlier you check in, the closer to the front of the line you are. Although my flight leaves at 7 AM, it is now 11 AM the day before when it dawns on me that I haven't checked in yet. I get a sinking feeling in my heart and realize that although I put an appointment on my calendar to check-in earlier this morning, I failed to set an alarm to remind me. So I check in for my flights on my iPhone and receive a message that "the maximum number of online boarding passes has been issued. Please obtain a boarding pass at the airport." This is the first time I've forgotten to check in for a Southwest flight immediately after I'm eligible.

I have a flashback to a week ago when I was standing in line to board the flight down here. I distinctly remember thinking, "Who are the people who are in the last group, C? Why wouldn't they check in right away?" I feel a bit superior to them, while happily standing in my "A" group, towards the front of the line. It's not that I need to be first; I just don't want to be last. I want to make sure there is a spot in the overhead bin for my luggage, so I don't have to wait for it at the baggage claim after my flight.

Now at the airport on the day of my departure, I stand at the check-in kiosk to obtain my boarding pass since I checked in too late to receive it online. I am chagrined to be assigned a C26 boarding pass. I'm not last, but I will certainly be able to see the last person from there! Feeling like a loser, I take the boarding passes from the kiosk and head toward my gate. I feel my cheeks flush hot with embarrassment and feel as if I'm being taught a lesson about pride. I feel like my grade school teacher has just called me up to her desk to give me a lecture about playing well with others.

It is so easy to feel superior to others and not even realize we're thinking condescending thoughts. Often this starts out as a series of sarcastic comments to a friend or spouse and ends up being a bad habit. For instance, when someone cuts me off in traffic or makes a left-hand turn from the right-hand lane or when someone walks down the aisle of the plane bumping each person they pass with the end of the carry-on hanging off their shoulder. Or, in this instance, thinking the folks standing in the C line are disorganized or lazy. Now I see my judgment staring back at me. I'm in the C line. I don't know what is going on in anyone else's life, the challenges they are having. Most likely, their challenges are more and greater than mine. Perhaps they are carrying a heavier load and their position in line isn't a high priority. My perspective needs to change. My thoughts need to change from, "What's wrong with them?" to "What's wrong with me?" How can I increase my focus on how to be more like the Christ, and less like the world, too focused on comparing myself with others.

Dear Lord, Please help me to change my spirit of judgment and superiority. Humble me and soften my heart to love strangers. Open my eyes to see that comparison isn't helpful, and help focus my eyes on You instead of on others. Amen.

THE BIG STICK

*Lean on, trust in, and be confident in the Lord
with all your heart and mind and do not rely
on your own insight or understanding.
In all your ways know, recognize, and acknowledge Him,
and He will direct and make straight and plain your paths.*

Prov 3:5-6 AMPC

While staying on the Amalfi coast with my husband several years ago, we decided to take a hike up into the hills so we could enjoy the countryside and see the view from the top of the hills there. If you've ever been to the Amalfi coast, you know that the entire area is a series of mountains. Towns are built into the hillsides and are crisscrossed with stairs. In fact, there were six flights of stairs down to our villa from the closest road. I knew that this hike would push my fitness limits. I'd already been having some knee trouble during our visit, and I wasn't sure how my knees would like hiking up and down a relatively steep and rocky hill.

As we started our walk, we entered a sparse forest, a rocky path of stairs, often with a steep rock wall on one side and an abrupt drop-off on the other side. We came to a pen meant to hold sheep, made from rough logs. Leaning against one edge was a thick sturdy walking stick, which probably doubled as a staff to persuade the sheep to go the right way. I wondered if it might be ok if I borrowed it. The steps were very steep and not kind on my knees. I decided to chance it, thinking that I would return it on the way back down. What a blessing that stick was! I could completely lean into it. Using it as a third leg, I allowed it to take some of the stress off my knees.

We made it to the top, stopping to admire the view, enjoy a snack and some water, and relax before the long descent. The place we took a break was right next to a large iron cross erected at the top of the hill we'd just climbed and overlooked the towns below. As we looked out across the rest of the peninsula, with the mountains stacked against one another receding in a fading blue haze, and across the water to the island of Capri, I was reminded that God made it possible for me to get to this summit and time of respite.

Only through leaning on Him can I make it to mountain top experiences in my life, and make it through the valley experiences stronger and trusting God more with each step.

Now that we'd made it to the top, we still had to get back down. Those of you who are hikers know it is often more challenging and dangerous to descend a mountain than to climb it because of the possibility of slipping and falling. I used that big stick even more on the way down, putting my full weight on it when the steps were too high for me to go down without aid.

That big stick is a great reminder that God is always there for us to lean on, helping through the rough spots on our journey. He enables us to do things we could not do on our own. We just need to realize and accept our weaknesses, share them with God, then reach out to receive His help. It is always available, just waiting for us to confess our inability to handle situations on our own.

Dear Lord, Help me to realize my need for You in all situations. Make it clear to my heart mind that I am inadequate for the task. Open my heart and my lips to confess to You my deep and ever present need for Your help. Thank You for always being right next to me, waiting for me to reach out for Your loving hand. Amen.

HOPE IN THE STORM

The Lord is my rock and my fortress and my deliverer,
my God, my rock, in whom I take refuge, my shield,
and the horn of my salvation, my stronghold.

PSALM 18:2

’ve taken a mini-vacation and headed up north to a little cabin on the lake. I was outside walking the tree-lined roads this morning, hours before the big snowstorm headed our way is forecasted to hit with almost a foot of snow. Spring is right around the corner. We have been having temperatures in the forties and fifties lately, which is pretty warm for pre-spring weather in northern Michigan. The wind is whipping around the bare branches of the trees and causing a roaring sound all around me. Any remaining dry leaves are rustling ominously. I feel the impending storm in my bones, like an imminent disaster. I quicken my steps in an effort to reach home sooner.

As I'm hurrying back to the warmth of the cabin, a clear crisp tweet of a bird singing a sweet song cuts through the growing cacophony, like an auditory ray of sunshine punching through a slate gray sky. This song, heard in early spring, foretells of the new life and warm temperatures to come. My heart quickens with momentary hope. Now I've stopped in my tracks, expectantly looking around in the trees to see if I can identify the bird singing the song.

That beautiful bird song reminds me that although trials may be headed my way, or I may already be in the midst of them, they only last for a season. And even in the middle of that season, I can experience hope and joy. I need to remember that God has it all under control. He is in charge. He has a plan for my life. I need not fear. In fact, the Bible has many verses reminding me not to be afraid. Isaiah 41:10 says "So do not fear, for I am with you; do not be dismayed, for I am your God. I will strengthen you and help you; I will uphold you with my righteous right hand." That sweet bird song is a promise of spring just as God's reassuring Word in Isaiah reminds me of His promise always to be there holding my hand through each trial. This verse is written in the present tense. He is with me, implying He is with me always, in every present moment. His Word is a promise for me while I am in this world and a pledge to take me into the next. This life is a trial, but God's promise is that I will be with Him in eternity one day. I just have to stay the course.

When I am feeling stressed out, tense and anxious, I've found the most helpful action I can take is to stop whatever I'm doing and find a quiet place alone to shut out the noise of the world while I talk with God. I simply tell him what is on my mind and heart, and tell Him I can't do it alone. I examine my heart and ask Him to extend to me whatever my heart needs to stay the course: His love, grace, peace, patience, and perseverance. I end my prayer asking God to increase my faith and trust, and thank Him for this present trial which is drawing me closer to Him.

Dear Lord, I praise You for Your awesome power, for the invigorating beauty of a snow storm, for the wind, and for warm, safe shelter. I praise You for reminders of Your sovereign control in the middle of difficult times, for Your word that reminds me of Your eternal presence. Thank You for sending blessings when times are tough. Open my eyes and heart to see them. Amen.

SNORKELING

*That is what the Scriptures mean when they say,
"No eye has seen, no ear has heard, and no mind has imagined
what God has prepared for those who love him."*

1 CORINTHIANS 2:9 NLT

The first time I snorkeled was in Hawaii. I borrowed a mask and a snorkel from a friend. I wear corrective lenses normally so I could not see clearly, but I could see clearly enough to observe the colorful wonders in the ocean and realize it was unlike anything I had seen before. If I swam really close to things, they would be in focus. I saw amazing plants that moved with the water, colorful corals of all shapes and sizes, interesting fish and graceful sea turtles. I also saw Hawaii's state fish, the incredibly colorful and detailed Humuhumunukunukuapua'a; a spectacular name for a spectacular fish.

Although friends had tried to explain what snorkeling was like and how interesting it was, I had not been able to imagine what it was like until I tried it for myself and then it became clear. Sometimes words cannot explain an experience well enough to do it justice.

I love being under the water and seeing that world which is so different from ours. I feel proected, like the water is a comforting blanket; that I've left all my problems behind me, and my heart is at peace.

Getting to know God and Christ is much like that first experience I had snorkeling. I can see the rough outlines of who God is. And can understand His characteristics a little, but not fully. Everything is fuzzy and it is like seeing through a glass darkly. 1 Corinthians 13:12 says, "Now we see things imperfectly, like puzzling reflections in a mirror, but then we will see everything with perfect clarity. All that I know now is partial and incomplete, but then I will know everything completely, just as God now knows me completely." Once we die and go to heaven we will be able to see God clearly and will experience what we now can only begin to imagine.

Each time I snorkel I see new things, and each experience leaves me yearning to return. When I spend quality quiet time alone with God and His peace settles over me, I catch a glimpse of what I imagine heaven will be like – closeness with God – each experience leaves me yearning to return to that special place.

Christ said He was leaving to prepare a place for us. I think we can imagine the wonders of the ocean as a pale and partial foretaste of the wonders to come in heaven that God is preparing for us. I suspect we will encounter new wonders and experiences every day, forever.

I don't know about you but I cannot wait to get to heaven. Today's media and images of heaven are flat and boring. I think I would be bored if heaven's main activity was sitting around on a cloud singing, or strumming a harp. If you have been pursuing a relationship with Christ and search the Scriptures for clues about heaven, I suspect you will find that although we may have an unclear picture of what awaits us, it will be beyond our wildest imagining.

If you are curious about what awaits you in heaven, I recommend Randy Alcorn's book, *Heaven*. He has a full-length book and also a smaller booklet with highlights from his book if you want just the highlights to whet your appetite.

> *Dear Lord, Thank You for the beauty of the sea and Your immense creativity. I enjoy Your creation and marvel and its diversity. It makes me long to be with You in Eternity. Please give me patience and perseverance to continue furthering Your mission here on Earth, and open my eyes to the joys of Your creation daily. Amen.*

GRACE

Do not judge, and you will not be judged.
Do not condemn, and you will not be condemned.
Forgive, and you will be forgiven.

LUKE 6:37 NIV

learned a lesson in judging and grace today. Most Christians know the verses in Matthew 7, "Judge not that ye not be judged…" and yet adhering to it is so hard. It's so easy to sit back and judge others who get in my way, as pushy, and to misread someone's shyness as being stuck up. When these ideas are creeping into my thoughts, I need to learn to extend grace to others.

When spending an extended amount of time on fairly small ship, confined with 150 other passengers, inevitably I'm going to form opinions about many of them before ever exchanging words. The woman who gives me a strange look may just be trying to place my face – she thinks she knows me. The person who doesn't say hello back to my greeting may be hard of hearing or deep in thought when I said hello. I shouldn't be quick to take offense. The key is to get to know them and always to assume the best. Extend grace. Why is it that when someone is a stranger it's easier to believe the worst of him or her, but as a friend, to think the best? As soon as I form some reference point with them, such as a common interest or hometown, all of a sudden they become this "known entity," and the trait I thought I saw in them evaporates into thin air like vapor.

Just imagine the incorrect impressions you've given of yourself when you haven't been aware of your expression! I know my face is an open book. I would shudder to know what bad impressions I've made on others. When I think of that, it reminds me to extend God's grace to others the way God continually extends His grace to me.

All of us sin and fall short of the glory of God. None of us is perfect. We are all rude or inconsiderate at some point. It's my goal to work on believing the best of strangers. Give them the benefit of the doubt, extend grace. Maybe the slow driver in front of you is elderly, and this is the one time each week they venture out to purchase groceries because they have no one else to do it for them. Perhaps the person who cut you off on the highway just had a fight with their spouse, and they're upset. Possibly that fellow traveler is painfully shy and uncomfortable in social situations. Whatever it is, if we can control our thoughts, we've won more than half the battle, because what we think and believe becomes our reality.

Remember that Jesus has forgiven all our sins, and extend that grace to others who may appear inconsiderate. If you've encountered someone on your travels, with whom you are feeling at odds and you have an opportunity to talk with them, take it. Get to know them and foster love and grace with the people you encounter on your travels and in your life.

Dear Lord, In this busy, crazy world I am often offended by such little things, thinking negative thoughts about those I hardly know. Please help me to extend grace daily in situations where it would be easy to think negatively. Give me the heart to reach out to others and care about them instead of being annoyed with them. Amen.

CAPTIVATED

Then Christ will make his home in your hearts as you trust in him.
Your roots will grow down into God's love and keep you strong.
And may you have the power to understand, as all God's people
should, how wide, how long, how high, and how deep his love is.
May you experience the love of Christ, though it is too great to
understand fully. Then you will be made complete with all
the fullness of life and power that comes from God.

EPHESIANS 3:17-19 NLT

Last summer we took the children on an RV trip out west to see the sights. One of our stops was at the Grand Canyon. We parked our rented RV and then walked out to the rim. Neither the kids nor my husband had ever seen it. As we approached the edge and could start seeing down into the canyon, our 14 year-old son grew quiet, an odd phenomenon, and the unimpressed look on his face changed to one of awe and wonder which stopped him in his tracks, at least for a few seconds. Then he was off like a rocket, jumping from one rock to the next, trying to get as close to the edge as possible without falling in. Later that evening, he wanted to head back down to the brink to just sit, something he rarely does. My husband and I followed several minutes later and were surprised to see him quietly sitting cross-legged, captivated by the beauty and grandeur of the Grand Canyon. I think it takes a while sitting in solitude and taking in the scenery to comprehend just how big, and deep, and long, and wide it is. It takes something pretty impressive to captivate our young teenage son for long. I'm just tickled that the Grand Canyon impressed him.

I believe that God, in the form of Christ, died on the cross as a substitute for me and my sins, and that He rose again afterward, and that because of His sacrifice I am reconciled to God, able to talk directly with Him and will be with Him forever in Heaven. I've believed this most of my life. But it has also taken most of my life even to start to comprehend how wide, long, high and deep God's love is for me. Most days I hardly even scratch the surface of that understanding. It takes a lot of alone time talking with

Him, sitting and listening for His leading. Occasionally I get glimpse of this truth. Over my life I've seen many "God-incidents" happen. When I get the feeling I should call a friend, and they exclaim on the other end of the line that my timing couldn't have been better or when my husband feels called to arrange breakfast with an old friend, only to find out they really needed a friend to talk with urgently that day.

I've seen God's guiding hand leading me over and over throughout my life. Some people may dismiss these things as coincidences, but I know they are "God-incidents." Waking up to the realization of how God leads my life is akin to staring out at the Grand Canyon and beginning to discern the layers of rock and sediment that make up the earth's surface. I'm starting to see who God is and how He cares, specifically for me, in response to the things I tell Him and the things for which I ask Him. He isn't some remote god who helps us on an impersonal level. I am captivated by how He loves each one of us individually and craves to have a close relationship with us, closer than any human relationship we've developed. But we must trust Him first. Ephesians 3:17 says, "Christ will make his home in your hearts as you trust in him." Verse 19 says, "Then you will be made complete with all the fullness of life and power that comes from God." God completes us! He makes our lives full and gives us power.

Dear Lord, I know it is impossible while I am still on this earth to fully comprehend how much You love me, but please crack open that mystery a little from time to time to build my trust and faith in You. Instill in me the desire to know You more fully, to spend time with You, to share my heart with You, and to ask for Your guidance through each day. Amen.

LAST

For people will be lovers of self, lovers of money, proud, arrogant,
abusive, disobedient to their parents, ungrateful, unholy,

2 TIMOTHY 3:2

I was on a Southwest flight recently with my family. Although we had checked in pretty close to the initial time you can check in, 24 hours ahead, we were not in the "A" group. Because there were three of us who needed seats together, we found ourselves almost in the back of the plane. We walked past all the others who had taken seats up front. It's convenient to be up front because you don't have to lug your stuff as far, you're first off the plane, and if your flight arrives late, being first off gives you a better chance at making your next connection. Most everyone likes to be first. When I park, I look for the closest spot to the store entrance. When I'm boarding on other airlines, I like to be one of the first people queued up when my group is called so I can get situated in my seat quickly and with minimal hassle. When I exit an international flight, I like to be first to customs and immigration so I don't have to wait for a long time.

When our plane landed, the pilot made an announcement that there were problems with the jet bridge and that we would be deplaning from the rear of the airplane. I heard groans from the front of the plane as I heard cheers from the back. What an unexpected gift! Here we thought we'd be last off and we were going to be first instead! At the end of a long day, it was a welcome surprise.

God urges us not to be proud, arrogant or greedy. In our current culture, which values self-reliance and "getting what you've got coming to you," I find it very easy to fall into the habit of thinking "me first," or of only thinking of myself. Very often, when I'm in the grocery store, my primary goal is to get in and out of there as quickly as possible and at all costs. However, the costs involve me not being as gracious or as cordial as I could be. If I were to monitor the dialogue running through my head, some of the phrases running through it might be, "Hello! Pick an item and move on," or "It must be nice to have all that time to wander through the aisles at a leisurely pace," or "You're standing right where I want to be, hmm." You get the picture. I'm not focused on anyone else but myself.

At the grocery store is exactly where I have an opportunity to shine God's love and grace into the lives of others. I should be looking for opportunities to be salt and light. I've started focusing on others while I'm in public. When I find my thoughts motivated by self-gain, I work to reorient them. After saying a little prayer such as, "Lord Jesus, help me to put others first and to reflect Your love to others," I look for ways to assist others. If someone in line behind me has fewer items than I do or they have kids, I invite them to get in line ahead of me. I smile at others in the store and engage the clerks at the register and those folks who are bagging the groceries. I try to add a little levity to their day or distract them from the monotony of their jobs for a few minutes. God calls us to embody the characteristics of Christ in whatever we do.

Challenge yourself to be others-centered each time you are in public, especially when you are running errands on your own, during those times when it's easy to be self-absorbed instead of using each experience as an opportunity to shine God's light to others.

> *Dear Lord, When I'm rushing through my day, I'm often too focused on myself. Help me find ways to focus on allowing Your attributes to flow through me to others I encounter and make me aware of how I might help them. Amen.*

Moai

Be strong and courageous. Do not fear or be in dread of them,
for it is the Lord your God who goes with you.
He will not leave you or forsake you.

Deuteronomy 31:6 ESV

We are told that Easter Island is a land full of mystery. I've been intrigued by Easter Island for a long time and have wanted to visit for many years. It is one of the most remote islands in the world. It is a five-hour flight directly west of Santiago, Chile. I spent a week there and the Rapa Nui (Easter Islanders) don't think there is any mystery about their island. They know where their ancestors came from and they have explained why the extraordinarily heavy Moai were carved and how they were transported across the island.

The Rapa Nui believed that their ancestors' spirits possessed the power to come to their aid if necessary. Mostly, this belief was attributed to influential members of their clan such as chieftains. This belief led to the development of the Moai. When a tribal chief died, a Moai sculpture was ordered and was carved in the quarry on the outer edge of the Rano Raraku volcano. It was later transported to its village and placed on a ceremonial altar. However, the Rapa Nui believe that the more distant the relative, the less that relative would care about coming to their aid. So, every few generations they had to order another Moai to be sculpted and brought to their village to ensure protection. Eventually each Moai fell over, with their face in the dirt, or with their face looking up at the true God.

How full of joy I am that I never have reason to doubt God's protection. God is always with us, always wanting the best for us, throughout our lives. God's love isn't conditional on who we are or how closely related we are to Him. The Triune God can't be contained in any physical representation like an idol.

He has sent His Holy Spirit to live inside of each believer to help guide, comfort and help us. John 14:16 says, "And I will ask the Father, and he will give you another Counselor to be with you forever." The Greek word counselor is translated from means "one who is called alongside," and has the picture in it of one who is an encourager and one who prods. The Spirit also has the job of revealing truth to us, helping us to understand scripture in a way that is meaningful and clear. I often think of the Spirit in myself as my conscience, and this is true for believers. When I'm paying attention, the Spirit will cause me to feel uneasy if I am about to go the wrong direction or make the wrong choice.

When I start to worry about difficult circumstances that I don't feel I can deal with, Romans 8:38-39 (ESV) reassures me. "For I am sure that neither death nor life, nor angels nor rulers, nor things present nor things to come, nor powers, nor height nor depth, nor anything else in all creation, will be able to separate us from the love of God in Christ Jesus our Lord." This means that no matter what awful trial I am dealing with, God knows about it. He has either ordained it or allowed it to happen, in order to bring good out of it. There is no way to understand God's perspective on this. All I can do is trust that He is in control, and He is with me. This can feel almost impossible sometimes. But when I look back on the most difficult parts of my life I can see how God protected me, guided me through, and ultimately brought me out on the other side stronger and closer to Him. I have seen this again and again in my life.

> *Dear Lord, I thank You that You are the supreme God over everything that exists. Thank You for loving me so much that You protect and guide me each step of the way. Help me to be open to Your leading and prompting from Your Holy Spirit. Develop my trust in You, so that through the toughest times I still believe and trust that You have my best interests at heart, and will bring me safely to the other side, stronger and closer to You. Amen.*

TOUR GROUP

As the heavens are higher than the earth,
so are my ways higher than your ways,
and my thoughts than your thoughts.
ISAIAH 55:9 NIV

When I'm traveling, I like to be free to do what I want. I don't usually like being part of a group that has a detailed and time-bound itinerary. However, there are several upsides to being part of a tour. It is nice to have everything planned for you; to have meals provided, busses booked, and a leader who is in charge. I can trust they have it all under control, and I can just enjoy the scenery and the trip, and drink in all the surprises that cross my path without feeling like I'm in charge of how it turns out.

When I visited New Zealand with my mom several years ago, we arranged for a three-week tour. This way we could enjoy each other's company and simply enjoy our time together. Everything was planned for us, all we had to do was show up on time each day and get back to the bus on time during side trips. When the bus stopped at a roadside attraction, we could leave our belongings on the bus while we learned how kiwi fruits are raised, enjoy an afternoon tea that was already arranged for us, or browse at a local shop that made accessories out of possum fur. It is a real luxury not to be concerned with all the little details that are part of a trip.

One afternoon we arrived at our hotel only to find that all of us had been booked into smoking rooms when we'd all requested non-smoking rooms. My immediate reaction was to try to handle the situation myself, but I remembered all I had to do was let the tour group leader know there was a problem. I have a natural tendency to jump in and take control of a situation. This tendency started in school when teachers divided the class into several small groups to accomplish a task. That inclination plays against me when I need to mentally give over control to God, even though I know I'm never truly in control. I enjoy relying on myself. I got married late in life, and the necessitated self-reliance of living alone served me well for many years.

God is working to teach me a new way now; teaching me to trust Him and His way.

God is like our tour guide but instead of having the itinerary for a trip He has a plan for our lives, and it's better than any plan we could have constructed. I Corinthians 2:9 says, "But, as it is written, "No eye has seen, no ear has heard, and no mind has imagined the things that God has prepared for those who love him."" (ISV) He has it all under control. I am not in control although I often delude myself into thinking I am. I just need to trust that He is in control and let Him know when I experience a problem. Then I need to follow the itinerary and show up and pay attention to the surprises that God has planned for me along the way.

When something doesn't seem to go well during my travels or in life in general, I am not the one who has to fix it, He will. God did not design us to carry that burden. We have to trust Him with it and thank Him for the opportunity to grow our confidence in Him. This is often no easy task! If you're having trouble, thanking God for a particular challenge that is in your life right now, find a quiet spot, close your eyes and say aloud the following prayer.

> *Dear God, I trust You. Thank You for this trial. I don't feel like thanking You for it, and I don't like it, but I still trust You. Please give me Your strength, hope, perseverance, and courage to guide me through this challenge. Help me to allow You to control the situation, and open my eyes to Your guidance in it. Amen.*

TEATIME

*When I remember you upon my bed, and meditate on you
in the watches of the night; for you have been my help,
and in the shadow of your wings I will sing for joy.
My soul clings to you; your right hand upholds me.*

PSALM 63:6-8

In order to keep on my feet and be somewhat coherent yesterday, I consumed vast amounts of tea. I'm in Ireland with my long-time friend, Beth, and the rigors of travel seem to have taken the wind out of our sails. Tea, here, appears to be something of an art form. Nowhere in the states have I ever tasted tea as it tastes in this part of the world (Britain, Scotland, Ireland). It's just divine! I think it has something to do with slowing down. I believe that it is made with time as a consideration.

We tend to try rushing through life by shortening the time it takes to do things such as eating fast food picked up from drive-through windows. Anything that is faster must be better, right? Well, when it comes to tea, faster is not better. Pre-packaged, over-processed, over-packaged, is not better. When I make a cup of tea at home in my travel mug and rush off with it in the car while I drive, it isn't relaxing or even inviting.

I can see why people here in Ireland are committed to their tea and their daily tea time. It's that good! A good pot takes a little time. But it is so worth the wait. So much worth the wait that it is a shame to rush the experience. You must just sit back, take a deep breath and settle into your tea. It's not just a cup of hot liquid, it is a time of day, a relaxing experience, invigorating for the senses, and it is soul-renewing. To experience the most from having tea, you must work at it, dedicate time to it, and possibly even set aside time for it where nothing else happens during that period.

Another soul renewing activity is spending time with God. But most of us don't take time on a regular basis to do it or to do it consistently enough to reap the benefits of it. I am guilty of trying to rush my time alone with God. I try to squeeze it in between the time I wake up and the time I need to get out of bed. Often that time is filled with extra sleep as I succumb to a comfortable bed and the need for more shuteye.

When I set aside time to spend alone with God, I get glimpses of how good this "chair time" can be, and I start looking forward to it. These glimpses often occur when I pour out my heart to Him, thanking Him for the abundant blessings He showers me with and petitioning Him to intercede on behalf of others in my life who need help, guidance or hope. I see how it positively impacts my days and weeks. I feel closer to God and call on Him for help throughout my day. I can see more easily how scripture applies to my life and can apply those lessons personally. Joy creeps into my life in surprising ways and even during difficult seasons.

So, what are you waiting for? Maybe combining teatime with chair time is not a bad idea! Sit back, relax, take a deep breath and settle into spending time in the presence of your Lord. Quiet your mind. Sit quietly. It's not just a quiet time, it is an experience, and is soul renewing. Praise God for who He is, praise His blessings in your life, praise Him for the trials that bring you closer to Him and leave you with the knowledge that He is always with you, step by step, protecting and guiding if you will listen to his prompting.

> *Dear Lord, I thank You for the ability to speak directly and personally to You. Work in my heart and my will to foster the practice of daily spending quiet "chair time" in Your presence. Allow me to open my heart to You, and tell You all my concerns and troubles, even if it doesn't sound good and I don't have a positive attitude about it. I want to be real with You. Grow my trust in and dependence on You. When I drift away from our daily talks, draw me back in. Amen.*

Acknowledgements

This book is a product of some of the adventures and trials God has used as opportunities for growth in my life. I've taken lessons I've learned from traveling, and with God's help, distilled His life lessons and truths into these devotions.

To my husband, Rob, my whole life is enriched because of your ongoing encouragement and love. I treasure living life with you!

To my loving parents, who poured out their living faith into me from the time I was born. They gave me the firm foundation in Christ from which my faith continually grows.

I praise the Lord for His abundant blessings in my life, and for the lessons He teaches me every day. Thank you Lord, so much, for enabling me to capture, in writing, some of the lessons You have taught me. Please use these devotionals to bless each reader with Your wisdom, empower them to apply these lessons to their lives, and to continually grow closer to You.

ABOUT THE AUTHOR

Laura Vae Gatz is a writer, photographer, traveler and follower of Jesus. In 2011 Laura published **Africa Via Antarctica**, the tales and photographs from her two-month, around-the-world, sabbatical. **Beach Devotions** was her first devotional book, followed by **Autumn Devotions**. Both are available on Amazon.com.

Laura lives with her husband, Rob, on the edge of a wetland in the country, near Grand Rapids, Michigan.

If you enjoyed this book, please consider writing a review at Amazon.com or on Goodreads. Thank you!

65465485R00044

Made in the USA
Middletown, DE
27 February 2018